animals**animals**

Pigs and Hogs

by **Steven Otfinoski**

mc **Marshall Cavendish**
Benchmark
New York

Thanks to Donald E. Moore III, associate director of animal care
at the Smithsonian Institution's National Zoo, for his expert reading of this manuscript

Marshall Cavendish Benchmark
99 White Plains Road
Tarrytown, New York 10591-5502
www.marshallcavendish.us

Library of Congress Cataloging-in-Publication Data

Otfinoski, Steven.
Pigs and hogs / by Steven Otfinoski.
p. cm. — (Animals, animals)
Summary: "Provides comprehensive information on the anatomy, special
skills, habitats and diet of pigs and hogs"—Provided by publisher.
Includes index.
ISBN 978-0-7614-3971-4
1. Swine—Juvenile literature. I. Title. II. Series.
SF395.5.O84 2009
636.4—dc22
2008020899
Photo research by Joan Meisel

Cover photo: Arco Images/Steimer, C./Alamy

The photographs in this book are used by permission and through the courtesy of:
AP Images: 30, 31. *Alamy*: Renee Morris, 4; Penny Boyd, 10; Arco Images GmbH, 13, 14, 28; Colin Edwards, 23;
tbk.media.de, 25; Photos 12, 38. *Animals Animals - Earth Scenes*: Robert Maier, 26. Corbis: Frank Lukasseck, 1;
Haruyoshi Yamaguchi, 7; Owen Franken, 16; Peter Worth, 18; Macduff Everton, 32; DLILLC, 34; Frank May/dpa, 37.
Getty Images: AFP, 36; James Marshall/jmpx.com. *Minden Pictures*: Foto Natura, 8; Pete Oxford, 12.
Peter Arnold Inc.: Biosphoto/Klein J.-L. & Hubert M.-L., 20. *Photo Researchers, Inc.*: Victor Habbick Visions, 35.
SuperStock: age fotostock, 11; Eureka Slide, 22.

Editor: Joy Bean
Publisher: Michelle Bisson
Art Director: Anahid Hamparian
Series Designer: Adam Mietlowski

Printed in Malaysia
1 3 5 6 4 2

Contents

 A Misunderstood Animal

Pity the poor pig! Few animals are as misunderstood as the pig. Most people think pigs are dirty, lazy, and stupid. In fact, pigs are clean, active, and some of the most intelligent animals.

How did the pig become so misunderstood? A lot of it has to do with one strange fact. Pigs have no sweat *glands*. Sweat cools off the bodies of other animals and humans. The only way a pig can cool off is to cover its skin with water or mud. Mud is the best covering because it also protects a pig's sensitive skin from the burning rays of the sun. So pigs do not like to be dirty—they just like to stay cool. In every other way, pigs are extremely clean animals. For example,

Pigs may seem like messy animals, but they just roll around in the mud to stay cool.

they pick the farthest place from where they eat and sleep to go to the bathroom.

If you saw a pig cooling off in mud, you might think it was a lazy animal. But pigs have a lot of energy. They spend much of their time *rooting* in the ground for plant roots and insects to eat.

And pigs are actually quite smart. Many scientists think pigs are the fourth most intelligent animals after chimpanzees, dolphins, and elephants. For example, pigs can be taught the same tricks you can teach a dog. They can be trained to respond to the command "sit" and to walk on a leash. They can even be house trained. A baby pig can learn to respond to its name just two to three weeks after birth. For these reasons, pigs make excellent pets.

Most pigs are not kept as pets, though. They are raised on farms and sold for meat. Pig meat is called pork. About one-fourth of all animal meat eaten in the United States is pork.

The wild *boar* is the closest relative of the *domestic* pig. About eight thousand years ago, people in Europe and Asia first started

Did You Know . . .
About half of all the world's pigs live in China. Other top pig-producing places are Europe, the United States, Brazil, and Vietnam.

Some pigs can be kept as pets, and they can even be walked on a leash like a dog.

to domesticate and raise pigs. But not all pigs are domestic. Wild hogs and boars are found in Africa, Asia, and Europe. *Peccaries* are distant pig relatives that live in the wild in Mexico and Central and South America.

These wild boar piglets are close relatives to the domestic pig.

Species Chart

◆ The Poland China pig is one of the most popular *breeds* of pigs in the United States. It was developed not in Poland or China, but in southern Ohio in 1860. It is a *crossbreed*—an offspring of different pig breeds. The Poland China has a long and muscular body. It is black with white spots on its face, tail, and feet. This breed is the leading pork-producing pig in the nation.

A female Poland China pig.

The African forest hog is the largest of all species of wild pig. It can grow to be 6.5 feet (2 meters) long and can weigh as much as 600 pounds (270 kilograms). The forest hog lives in the jungles of western and central Africa. It is black and has long, pointed ears. This pig is an *herbivore*, or plant eater. It lives in *herds* of up to twenty hogs.

An African forest hog.

Vietnamese pot-bellied pigs.

◆ The Vietnamese pot-bellied pig is one of the smallest domestic pigs. It is about 2.5 feet (0.8 meters) long and weighs 75 to 150 pounds (34 to 68 kg). It is usually solid black, but can also be spotted. Originally from Southeast Asia, the pot-bellied pig is now a popular pet in the United States and other countries.

What is the difference between a pig and a hog? According to American livestock experts, a hog is an older domesticated pig weighing more than 120 pounds (54 kg). A pig is a young, immature hog. In common usage, however, the names are often used to mean the same thing. People also use a third word for pigs, *swine*.

Pigs are members of a large family of animals that includes cattle, deer, and peccaries. All these animals have hooves and an even number of toes on each foot. Pigs have four toes on each foot, but they walk on only two of those toes. It makes them look as if they walk on their tiptoes.

Pigs are one of the animals in the family that includes these peccaries.

A pig's tusks can help the animal dig for food and defend itself against enemies.

All pigs have large, stocky bodies and thick skin covered by bristly hairs. Their tiny tails can be straight or curled. A pig's large head ends in a long *snout*. This sturdy snout contains a big bone and other tough tissue. Pigs use their snouts to breathe, to smell, and to dig in the ground for food.

Pigs have a total of forty-four teeth. Their long *canine teeth* are called *tusks*. They use their tusks for digging and defending themselves. All pigs have tusks, but many farmers clip them off when a pig is young so the animal cannot hurt anyone or anything. Pigs have tiny eyes in relation to their body size, but they have excellent vision. However, they rely mostly on their keen sense of smell to find food.

13

2 A Hearty Appetite

In one area a pig's reputation is well earned. It is actually appropriate to call someone who eats greedily a pig. Pigs like to eat, and they will eat almost anything they can find. Most pigs are *omnivores*—animals that eat both plants and meat. If given the chance, pigs will devour everything from lizards and mice to tree bark and flowers. Pigs will eat *carcasses*—dead animals. And they will even eat birds if they can catch them.

Pigs and people have one thing in common when it comes to eating—they both like truffles. *Truffles* are a kind of fungus that grows underground. They are considered a *delicacy*. Truffles can be eaten whole or

Pigs love to eat, and most domestic pigs, such as these shown here, eat a mixture of meat, grain, vegetables, and fruit.

One of the ways pigs help humans is by sniffing out truffles.

used as a flavoring for other foods. In France and Italy, people use pigs to find and root out truffles. They train the pigs to find the truffle, but not eat it. This is another reason that pigs are really smart!

Farmers feed special pig chow to most domestic pigs. This feed contains animal *protein*, grains, plant protein, and other *nutrients*. Farmers also feed pigs regular snacks of fresh fruits and vegetables. Although their stomachs may be full, pigs will still root around in the ground for other food. It is in their nature to do so.

Domestic pigs live on farms in a *sty*. This is a covered pen with an open area where they can run around and be close to other pigs. Pigs are highly social animals, so they like being around other pigs and other animals. The only farm animals that pigs do not always get along with are dogs. Maybe pigs and dogs are too much alike. Both are highly intelligent and they compete for the company of people.

Pigs communicate with each other by making a series of oinks, grunts, and squeals. One pig grunt may sound much like another to you, but scientists have identified

Did You Know . . .
Pigs have bad manners when it comes to eating. At feeding time, they push and shove each other to get at food that the farmer puts in a feeder called a *trough*.

17

Pigs enjoy snacking on fresh fruits, such as apples.

more than twenty different kinds of sounds made by pigs, each having its own meaning. When a pig is content, it snorts softly. One kind of oink might mean, "I'm hungry!" But watch out when you hear a high-pitched, loud squeal! This is a pig telling the world that it is not happy at all. Pigs communicate with body language, too. They like to snuggle up with a friend in the sty and pigs will often sleep nose to nose.

3 Sows and Their Piglets

By the time pigs are about eight months old, they are able to mate and produce young. A female pig is called a *gilt* before she has her first babies. After she gives birth, she is called a *sow*. A male pig is called a boar. The sow carries her young inside her for about four months. Then she gives birth, a process called *farrowing* in pigs. An average *litter* is between six and twelve *piglets*, although there can be as many as twenty or more in one litter.

Pig farmers help domestic sows to care for their young. The farmer makes sure that the mother does not accidentally harm her piglets. The sow weighs

Piglets are born after their mother carries them for just four months.

much more than her newborn piglets and could roll over and crush them. To prevent this from happening, the farmer places the mother and young in a crate that is too small for her to roll over in. Some farmers build a special stall where the piglets can go when their mother is getting up or lying down. This also

Did You Know . . .
People can drink pig's milk. It has as many nutrients as cow's milk. Unfortunately, pigs are difficult animals to milk and few people try to milk them.

Piglets are very small when they are born and farmers take care to make sure the piglets's mother does not roll over onto them.

protects them from getting crushed. In wintertime, the farmer will hang a heater over the crate to keep the mother and piglets warm.

The little piglets are chubby and ready to play. The piglets learn the sound of their mother's voice quickly and come running to feed on her milk through her *teats*. The piglets grow quickly on their mother's milk. In just three weeks, each piglet's weight triples from about 3 pounds (1.4 kg) to about 10 pounds (4.5 kg). The piglets are *weaned* from their mother's milk when they are four to eight weeks old. By that time, they will weigh about 35 pounds (15.7 kg). That is ten times their birth weight. No other farm animal grows that rapidly. Often they are weaned quicker when a substitute for sow's milk is fed to them. A weaned young pig is called a *shoat*. Once the mother's young pigs are weaned, the sow may then mate again and have another litter. Most sows average two litters a year.

Many shoats are sent to other farms for fattening up. When they are ready for market, the young pigs are killed for their meat. This often takes place from four to seven months after birth. Large, industrialized pig farms often cut short the time a mother has with her piglets. Living quarters for the pigs are often cramped and dirty. Animal rights groups, such as People for the Ethical Treatment of Animals (PETA), have fought for better and more humane conditions for sows and their piglets. If they are not sold for meat, pigs can live for nine to fifteen years.

Wild pigs do not mate until they are one year old. Boars will fight fiercely over a female at mating time, which is usually in December. The winner will become her mate. Once pregnant, the wild sow separates herself from the herd. She builds a nest for her young out of small tree branches and grass. The piglets are born four months later, about the same as

Two male wild boars fight in order to determine who will mate with a female.

A female wild boar stays close to her young after they are born.

domestic pigs. After only a week or two, the wild piglets will leave the nest to look for food. Although they continue to drink their mother's milk for three months, they are able to eat solid food, such as worms, after just two weeks.

The young piglets have a striped coat of hair for the first six months of life. The stripes help them to hide in brush and not be seen by *predators*. After that time, they grow an adult, solid-colored coat of hair. The piglets will remain with their mother until she gives birth again the following spring. By then, they are about a year old.

4 Pig Troubles

Pigs in the wild are usually not killed for their meat as are many domestic pigs, but they face other dangers. Wild boars in Africa and Asia are the *prey* of tigers, wolves, and other large predators.

Boars and wild hogs flee from predators, but if they are caught by surprise or cornered they will fight fiercely. A male will lower his head like a bull and charge the enemy. Then he twists his curved tusks upward to *gore* the attacker. Females do not have tusks, but they will bite an attacker with their sharp teeth in order to protect themselves.

Most pigs have more to fear from disease than from predators. Pigs tend to get many illnesses.

In the wild, pigs face a number of dangers, including being hunted by wolves.

Diseases that attack the lungs, such as bronchitis and pneumonia, can be deadly to a pig. The germs enter their small lungs and make breathing difficult.

Many disease-carrying insects and *parasites* thrive on pigs. Worms can infect a pig's digestive tract. After

Did You Know . . .

Pigs are one of the few animals their size that can survive the bite of a poisonous snake. The snake's fangs often cannot reach the pig's bloodstream, which lies below a thick layer of fat, to inject their *venom*. This renders the venom less deadly.

A medical worker disinfects a pig farm in China, where a disease was infecting their pigs.

This pig is being vaccinated against disease in China.

the pig is killed for meat, these worms will survive if the meat is not cooked thoroughly. Then they will invade the body of the person who eats the meat. This can result in the disease *trichinosis.*

Pigs can be *vaccinated* to prevent them from getting some diseases, such as cholera and swine flu. Swine flu rarely spreads from pigs to humans. However, an outbreak in China in 2005 killed more than forty people and made more than two hundred others sick. Scientists believe this and other recent human outbreaks of swine flu in Asia have been caused by people and pigs living close to each other in crowded villages and towns.

31

5 Pigs and People

The eight-thousand-year-old relationship between pigs and people has benefited people more than pigs. Unlike milk cows, horses, goats, and some other domesticated animals, pigs have been bred and raised primarily for meat.

Pig meat gets made into ham, bacon, sausage, and pork chops. Pigs' feet and knuckles are pickled and eaten. In some cultures, pigs' snouts, brains, tongues, and even their *intestines* are considered delicacies. In the American South, fried pigs' intestines are called chitterlings. Jewish people and Muslims, however, view the pig as an unclean animal. Their religion forbids them to eat pork products.

This high-tech farm in Iowa automatically monitors feeding schedules for pigs and the building temperature.

Pigskin is turned into leather and used to make belts, jackets, shoes, and gloves. Tough pig hair is used as the bristles in hairbrushes and also as stuffing for everything from mattresses to baseball gloves. Pig fat is an ingredient in soap, candles, shaving cream, and even explosives. Pig blood is used in animal feed, medicines, and fertilizer. Even the pigs' bones are ground down to make fertilizer and glue.

The hair of a pig is coarse and is used as bristles in hairbrushes.

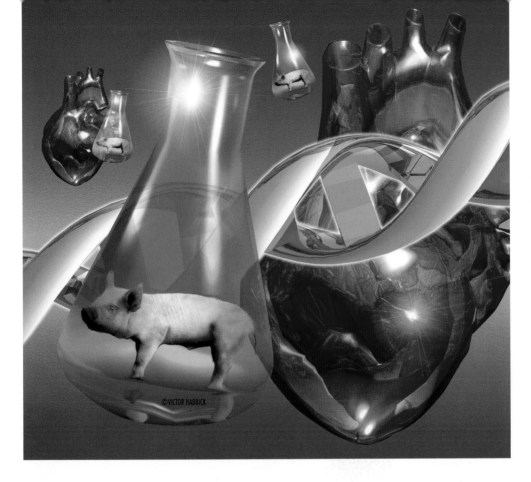

This computer illustration shows the concept of some organs from a pig can now be transplanted into humans.

More recently, people have found new uses for pigs in the field of medicine. Doctors discovered that a pig's internal organs are very similar to human organs. Parts of pig's organs, such as heart valves, can be *transplanted* into humans who need them. Also, by studying conditions such as heart attacks in pigs, doctors are learning how to better treat these diseases in humans. Chemicals produced by pigs' glands are being used to treat diseases such as arthritis and certain cancers in humans.

Few pigs were kept as pets in the United States until the mid-1980s. At that time, the first pot-bellied pigs were sold in this country. These dwarf pigs make great pets. They are much smaller than other pigs. They are quick learners, and they enjoy the company of humans. Like cats, they can be trained to use a litter box in a home. Like dogs, they require daily

A young boy in the Ukraine takes his pet Vietnamese pot-bellied pig for a walk.

walks on a leash. Pot-bellied pigs also need to be fed good nutritious food. Some pet owners feed them junk food that makes them overweight and is a threat to good health. Today, pot-bellied pigs are a popular pet in America.

Even though most domestic pigs are killed for their meat, they are not an *endangered* species. This has not always been true of wild pigs and hogs. The wild boar, for example, was hunted until it was *extinct* in England by about 1400. It still thrives, however, in other parts of Europe and Asia. The wild boar was recently reintroduced into the wild in England.

Wild pigs, like this sow and her piglets, were once an endangered species in England.

Some domestic pigs have escaped from farms and return to the wild. These pigs are called *feral* pigs. Feral pigs have caused problems in some areas, especially places like New Zealand and Hawaii where pigs are not native animals. Their rooting in the ground has damaged farmland and disturbed the natural environment. These countries are looking for ways to control the feral pig population.

Pigs are popular character in both books and movies. Babe, released in 1995, became a popular movie with both children and adults.

Pigs are fascinating animals. They are misunderstood by many people, but they still fascinate us. Pigs have appeared as characters in hundreds of children's stories, cartoons, and movies from *The Three Little Pigs* to *Babe*. Whether it is a farmer's pig in its sty or the cute pot-bellied pig that is somebody's pet, we owe a lot to pigs. Let's hear it for that clean and intelligent animal—the pig!

Glossary

boar—A male domestic pig of any age or a type of wild pig.

breed—Specific types of animal within the same species.

canine teeth—Pointed teeth used to tear food.

carcasses—The bodies of dead animals.

crossbreed—The offspring of two animals of different breeds or varieties.

delicacy—A fancy, often expensive food.

domestic—Suitable for living and working with humans.

endangered—Threatened by extinction.

extinct—Having died out, gone forever.

farrow—To give birth to pigs.

feral—Back in the wild after being domesticated.

gilt—A female pig that has not yet had babies.

glands—Organs that produce chemicals in the body.

gore—To pierce something, often with a tusk or a horn.

herbivore—An animal that eats only plants or plant materials.

herd—Groups of animals, such as wild hogs, that live together.

intestines—Long tubes below the stomach that digest food.

litter—A group of animals that an animal gives birth to at one time.

nutrients—Substances in foods that keep the body healthy.

omnivore—Animals that eats both plants and other animals.

parasites—Insects or other organisms that live on or inside an animal and depend on that animal for food or nutrients.

peccary—Hoofed animals that are distant relatives of the pig.

piglet—Baby pigs.

predator—Animals that preys on, or eat, other animals to survive.

prey—An animal that is hunted and eaten by other animals.

protein—A necessary substance supplied by foods such as meat, milk, eggs, nuts, and beans.

rooting—Tearing up the ground in search of food.

shoat—A pig that has just been weaned.

snout—A long nose.

sow—A female pig that has had young.

sty—A covered pen where pigs are kept.

swine—Another name for a pig or hog.

teats—The parts of female mammals that supply milk for young.

transplanted—Put into someone else's body.

trichinosis—A disease caused by parasitic worms that infect the intestines and the muscle tissue.

trough—A long, narrow container where animals feed.

truffle—Dark-colored underground fungi that humans consider a delicacy.

tusks—Long, curved teeth of pigs, elephants, and other animals.

vaccinated—Injected with a drug that helps prevent disease.

venom—Poison produced by some snakes.

weaned—A mammal that has moved from nursing from its mother to adult-style feeding.

Find Out More

Books

Dalgleish, Sharon. *Pigs* (Farm Animals). Philadelphia: Chelsea Clubhouse, 2005.

King-Smith, Dick. *All Pigs Are Beautiful.* Cambridge, MA: Candlewick Press, 2008.

Ray, Hannah. *Pigs* (Down on the Farm). Laguna Hills, CA: QEB Publishing, 2006.

Searl, Duncan. *Pigs* (Smart Animals). New York: Bearport Publishing, 2006.

Tait, Leia. *Potbellied Pig* (Caring for Your Pet). New York: Weigl Publishers, 2006.

Web Sites

The Joy of Pigs
www.pbs.org/wnet/nature/pigs/index.html

North American Potbellied Pig Association
www.petpigs.com

Pigs, A Sanctuary
www.pigs.org

Index

Page numbers for illustrations are in **boldface**.

About the Author

Steven Otfinoski is the author of numerous books about animals. He has also written *Koalas*, *Sea Horses*, *Alligators*, *Hummingbirds*, *Horses*, *Dogs*, and *Storks and Cranes* in the AnimalsAnimals series. Steve lives in Connecticut with his wife, a high school teacher and editor.